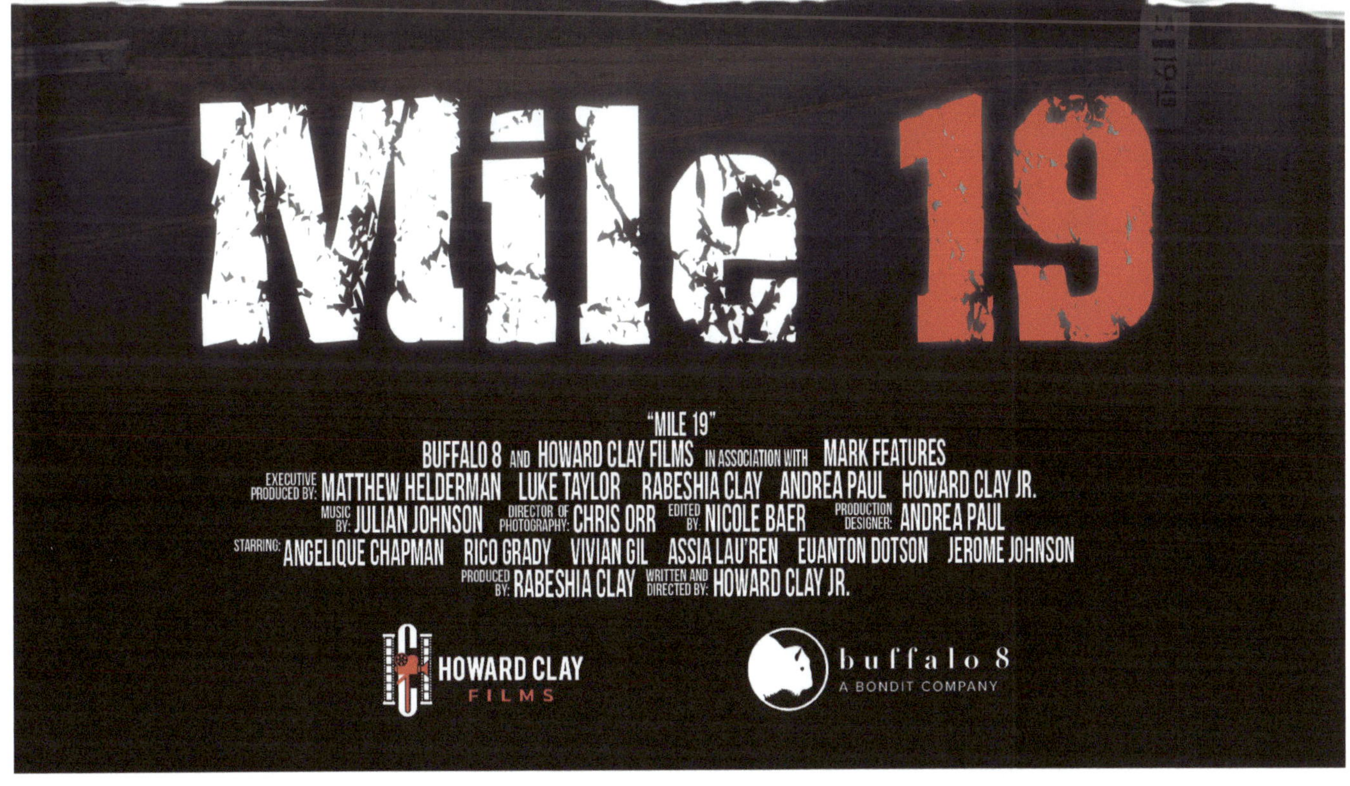
ANGELIQUE CHAPMAN
RICO GRADY
AF480328
WWW.HOWARDCLAYFILMS.COM
HOW FAR WOULD YOU GO TO HELP A STRANGER?
Mile 19
"MILE 19"
BUFFALO 8 AND HOWARD CLAY FILMS IN ASSOCIATION WITH MARK FEATURES
EXECUTIVE PRODUCED BY: MATTHEW HELDERMAN LUKE TAYLOR RABESHIA CLAY ANDREA PAUL HOWARD CLAY JR.
MUSIC BY: JULIAN JOHNSON DIRECTOR OF PHOTOGRAPHY: CHRIS ORR EDITED BY: NICOLE BAER PRODUCTION DESIGNER: ANDREA PAUL
STARRING: ANGELIQUE CHAPMAN RICO GRADY VIVIAN GIL ASSIA LAU'REN EUANTON DOTSON JEROME JOHNSON
PRODUCED BY: RABESHIA CLAY WRITTEN AND DIRECTED BY: HOWARD CLAY JR.
HOWARD CLAY FILMS
buffalo 8
A BONDIT COMPANY

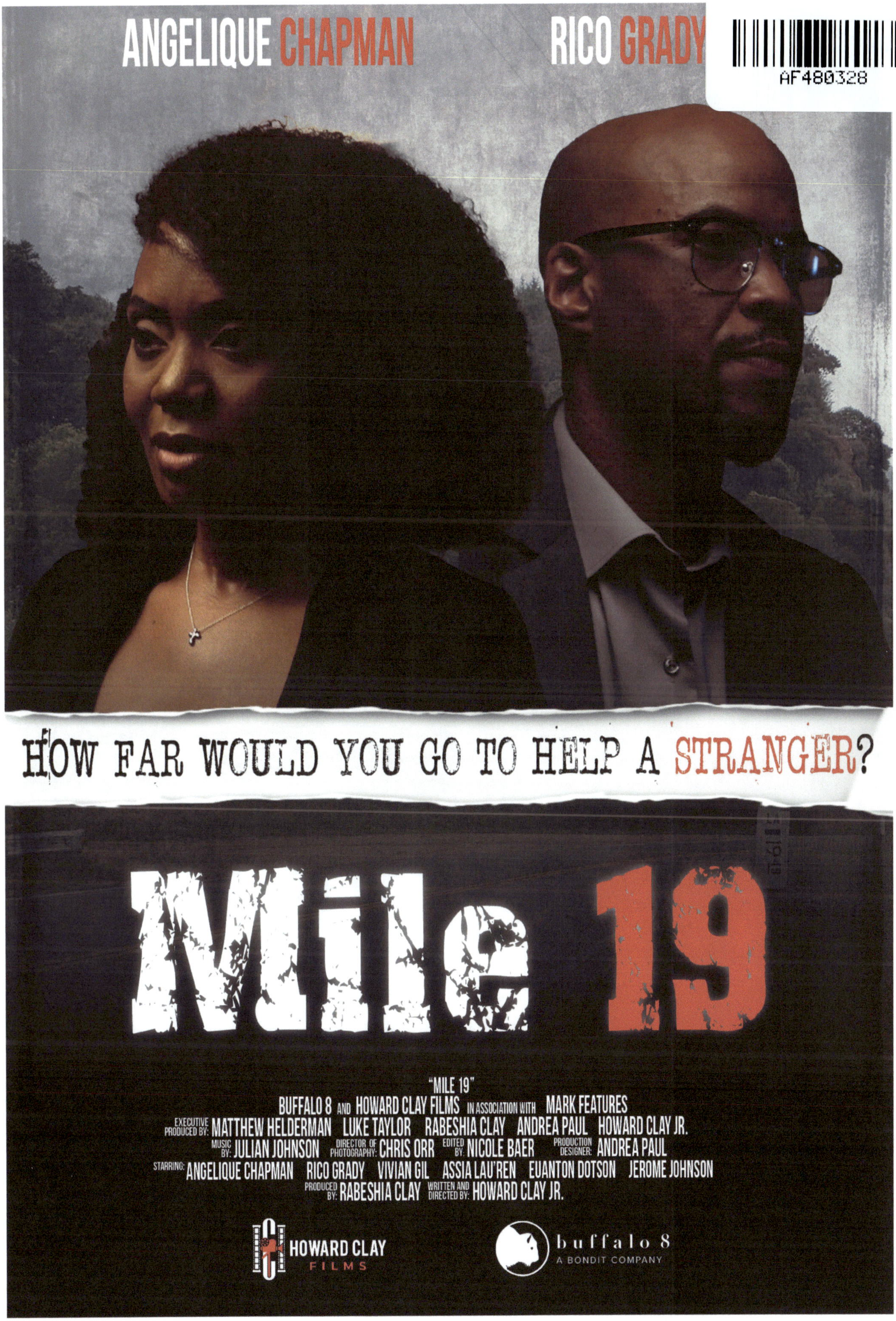

Founder/Publisher
Howard Clay Jr.

Editor-in-Charge
Desha Elliott

Art Director
Emmanuel Johnson

Entertainment and Lifestyle Director
Dvante Black

Marketing and Advertising Manager
Linda Clay

Media Relations Manager
LaTresa "Tree" Cunningham

Promotions Director
Jeffrey "Royce" Clay

Contributing Writers:
Michelle Burrage
Vincent Cunningham
Natyana Robertson
Angel Amos
Dr. Gillian Berry
Marcia Robinson
Desha "DrDesha" Elliott

South Region Advisor

Gloria Ishman

North Region Advisor

Pamela Thomas

Cincinnati Regional Ambassador

Myeeah Scott

Fort Valley State University Rep

Natyana Robertson

Contributing Editors
An Howard
Wymanette Castaneda

Photography
Tristan Ervin
Anthony Tyus
Larry Person
Drenay Evrett

Cover Photo & Design:
4th Park

Like a scab that never quite heals, racial tensions, and wealth disparities in the United States continue to scar many lives, and leaves many attempting to figure out what they can do to take their stand. I stand on the side of education and wealth all day. A moment that stood out to me while making this issue was an instance where I was asked to speak at a youth entrepreneur camp. I was initially asked to speak to these youth about branding and social media. What I observed from these youth at this camp as I and my other colleagues spoke, is how curious, innovative, and vocal these young people were. Now imagine if we took these minds and their energy and put it towards a particular problem plaguing a sizable population. I bet they would solve it! It's these same minds filled with curiosity and vigor, that we have to keep motivated, sharp, challenged, and put them in a position to get the knowledge they need to create limitless options for themselves. Pharrell Willams once mentioned that wealth is of the heart and mind. I believe that's where it starts, and it will continue to grow in the heart and the mind as long as that person is motivated. Let the pages of this issue inspire, motivate, and challenge you to obtain the education and wealth that you need to succeed.

About The Editor: Desha has created and delivered brand awareness and loyalty for over millions of consumers among many Fortune 500 Companies and small businesses under her Drdesha,LLC firm. In her years as social media creation and content creator manager, she has helped small businesses get millions of online impressions as well as help develop and implement marketing strategies for brand expansion..She is the author of the book, Hi My Name Is, a marketing guide for baby boomer entrepreneurs and professionals seeking a career change. As well as founder and CEO for the educational technology app, Playbook 7th Edition, which assist student athletes with improving their GPAs. For bookings, email drdesha@boss-emag.com.

So many people always have wondered where my passion lies. Is it education, is it entrepreneurs, is it money? The truth is, my passion is for the youth. Fortunately for me, I grew up with great parents and lots of strong male mentors to lead me on my way. But for most minority young men, this is not the reality that they are accustomed to. Then to top it off, it seems that this generation is bringing the minority struggle to the forefront from Kaepernick kneeling for injustice, to the unnecessary killings of minority citizens by public officers who are sworn to protect us. It seems like race and racism is right in your face. Nobody knows how this struggle and oppression will affect the youth of today but I have a pretty good idea. That is why my passion is with the minority young adults. They desperately need us to not only fight for justice and equality but to show them the RIGHT way to be successful in this society.

And for these reasons, and a few others, I have decided to make B.O.S.S. Magazine Inc, a 501c3 non-profit. Why? Becoming a non-profit gives us an opportunity to REACH MORE! Reaching more youth, more young adults, goes back to our mission of changing the media that our youth see today. I truly believe providing the most positive images and stories for our youth will give them a sense of direction and maybe even a sense of purpose. Our kids needs us today, not just to march, yell, and fight, but to explain our history correctly, and point them in the right direction. To not just tell them we are important, but show them. I believe in B.O.S.S, I believe in our mission and I believe the children are our future. Help me to get these magazines in the hands of our youth. Help me get them into more schools, more colleges, more libraries, and even more barber shops. Donate today and help me make BOSS Magazine the greatest minority educational magazine ever! Let's reach the youth together and change them one child at a time. Show them how to Be your Own Success Story, be a B.O.S.S!

Contact:
howard@boss-emag.com
Available for appearances and
speaking engagements.

"Making a Difference"

Kimario McFadden

B.O.S.S. got the opportunity to talk to Tampa Bay Buccaneer Safety #33 Kimario McFadden at his Youth Football Camp.

B: What is happens with participants that come to your football camp?

K: Right now at my camp we have myself and a few of my friends in the NFL that's going to be working with the youth on their skills and then we have educational sessions for the parents as well.

B: How important is education for a student athlete?

K: Education is so important, you can be the best athlete in the world. But if you do not have the right academics you won't be eligible to play.

B: What does it take to be successful?

K: It's going to take hard work, sacrifice, having belief in yourself and having Faith in God.

"Education is so important, you can be the best athlete in the world. But if you do not have the right academics you won't be eligible to play."

B.O.S.S.
Cover Story

Can these Millennials inspire a generation to spend different... They would say YES!

spendefy

Without a doubt this is one of the most exciting cover stories we have ever had. This business could quite possibly change the way we spend in our communities... forever.

BOSS: So let's start from the beginning, what is Spendefy?
Spendefy: Spendefy is a digital platform that makes it easy for consumers to discover amazing black-owned businesses in their city.
In light of all of the recent events happening in the black community and in our nation, our team at Spendefy wanted to be a part of the solution. Spendefy is a tech startup headquartered in Atlanta, GA. We have built a digital platform that leverages the power of consumerism for economic and social good by making it easy for consumers to discover amazing black-owned businesses in their city.
We're creating awareness and exposure for amazing blackowned businesses around the US.
After observing the ongoing lack of support for black-owned businesses in Atlanta and around the country, our team began to erect a plan to build solidarity between black-owned businesses and conscious consumers.

BOSS: Why have you chosen to dedicate yourself to this particular business/industry? What inspires you?
Spendefy: We have built a platform and a solution that addresses two problems - (1) a lack of exposure and respect for black-owned businesses and (2) a lack of education on the power of consumerism. We are awakening the sleeping consumer and inspiring them to Spend Different while elevating amazing black-owned businesses around the country. We believe BLACK businesses deserve to win! We believe we are carrying out the direct orders of Dr. King from his last speech, "I've Been to the Mountaintop". We believe Spendefy is a positive, scaleable and sustainable solution that everybody can believe in and support.

spendefy

BOSS: What makes your business/product unique?
Spendefy: Spendefy is UNIQUE because we are presenting black-owned businesses to the market in a way that has never been done before. We are making it easy to discover amazing black-owned businesses, and ultimately removing all excuses to supporting them. We are also raising the bar of conscious consumerism by encouraging our generation to Spend Different. No one else is doing this. We also have an amazing name, mission, vision, and tagline. Every aspect of Spendefy has been developed with extreme intention, scrutiny, research, and prayer. Even our logo has a defining meaning. The inspiration behind our logo comes from West African symbols known as Adinkra, which originated in Ghana – a beautiful West African country located on the Atlantic Ocean. We created our logo based on the West African symbol, NKONSONKONSON (pronounced "Kon-Son-Kon-Son"), which represents a chain link and the official symbol of unity and human relations. This symbol was originally used as "a reminder to contribute to the community; that in unity lies strength."

BOSS: You could have worked for anyone and would have been successful, why become an entrepreneur?
Spendefy: (Eldredge) I created my own business because when I work I am not working for me, I am working for my children's children. It is my desire to pay for my grandkids' education with the wealth created from Spendefy. If I was working a job, I would not be able to leave generational wealth behind.
(Antwon) Entrepreneurship gives you leverage. It provides access to more resources to do good in the world and solve real problems for real people. I want to play an active role in creating solutions that not only solves problems, but also creates jobs and opportunities for others. From my study of economics, business, capitalism, and influence, I believe it is what you own and control that determines the fate of yourself, your family, and your world.

BOSS: What is your business motto?
Spendefy: Our company motto is "Spend Different". We are encouraging a generation to Spend Different by leveraging the power of consumerism for economic and social good. We believe we can be the generation that celebrates the dynamic relationship between consumers and businesses; embracing the philosophy that true power derives from the union of the hand that gives with the hand that receives.

BOSS: If you could give other entrepreneurs up to five tips, what would they be?
Spendefy: Spend every day aiming to ask better questions and finding the right people with the answers. 2) Build systems around everything you do. You can only scale your business if you have an infrastructure that can sustain it. 3) Build a team of people who are smarter than you and who truly believe in your vision. Great teams are built when each team member can connect their head, heart and hands to your WHY. 4) Become obsessed with your product/service, your industry, your customer, and outworking/outsmarting your competitors. 5) Surround yourself with mentors, advisors and sponsors who can help you navigate your business faster and smarter.

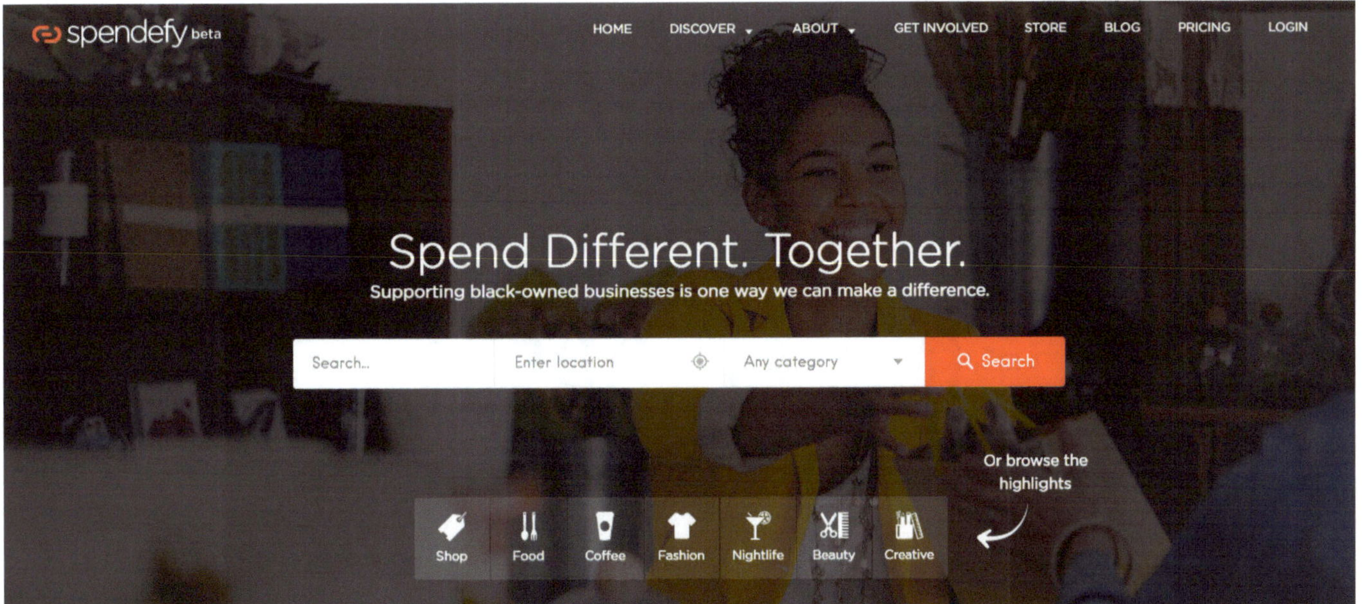

Spendefy Favorites™

Check out some of our favorite businesses in your city!

MADALI Hair

The ultimate in hair extensions.

Apple Butter Bakery

Specializing In Wedding & Custom Cakes

Stone Mountain Highway 5370, GA US

Davis Bozeman Law

Providing you access to experienced Attorneys when you need them most.

Flat Shoals Parkway 4153, GA US

BOSS: Has there been a piece of technology or software that has been a lifesaver to you?

Spendefy: Yes. Podio. We suggest all business owners look into using Podio. Podio is a cloud-based collaboration service for organizing team communication, business processes, systems, data, and content in project management workspaces. We literally run our entire company with Podio.

BOSS: When someone is talks to their friend about your business, what do you hope they say?

Spendefy: "Spendefy has made me a smarter and better consumer." "Spendefy has made me a smarter and better business owner." "Spendefy has made it easy for me to discover so many amazing black-owned businesses in my city." "Spendefy has helped my business get more exposure and more customers." "Spendefy is this DOPE movement of conscious consumers around the US and world." "I can literally do all of my shopping with black-owned businesses thanks to Spendefy."

INC. MY DREAM:
YOUNG BOSS CAMP

B.O.S.S. Magazine had an opportunity to speak at this year's Inc. My Dream Young Boss Camp. Students encountered the following through this camp:

1. Inspire confidence and clarify personal identity, purpose, and direction.

2. Teach problem-solving skills that can be used to bring practical solutions to issues in their communities.

3. Teach entrepreneurial skills that are transfer-able to the workplace and will be sustainable in any economy.

4. Focus on a holistic approach to small business development that focuses on character, leadership, team building, and communication skills.

5. Build the foundation to start businesses that can be fundable, profitable, and sustainable.

If you need any additional information on this camp please visit www.mykinsman.org/youth.

"Build the
foundation to start
businesses that
can be
fundable,
profitable,
and sustainable."

"Extra Points"

COACH HOWARD

Extra Points:
The Life of My Story — Coming Soon!

Coach Howard's upcoming book will take you through the wins and losses of his extraordinary life — including becoming the CEO of his own company, losing a $15 million fortune, and then rising again from the ashes. Extra Points: The Life of My Story will intrigue, inspire, and give hope to anyone who has a dream for their life.

Coach! Engage! Inspire! Motivate!
Having Coach Howard as your speaker will result in engaged audiences immediately after he speaks into the microphone. With over 300 games under his belt, coaching on and off the football field has afforded Coach Howard an uncanny presentation which always delivers as a crowd pleaser.

Ultimately, Coach Howard's folksy style achieves a truly WIN-WIN experience for audiences throughout the United States. A self-described "open book" Coach Howard uses his past fumbles to transform future wins to all in his presence. Storytelling, locker room rants and thousands of notes written over the years, lend best practices, mental mapping and a positive plan for WINNING.

Preorder your copy today!
http://www.extrapointsllc.com/

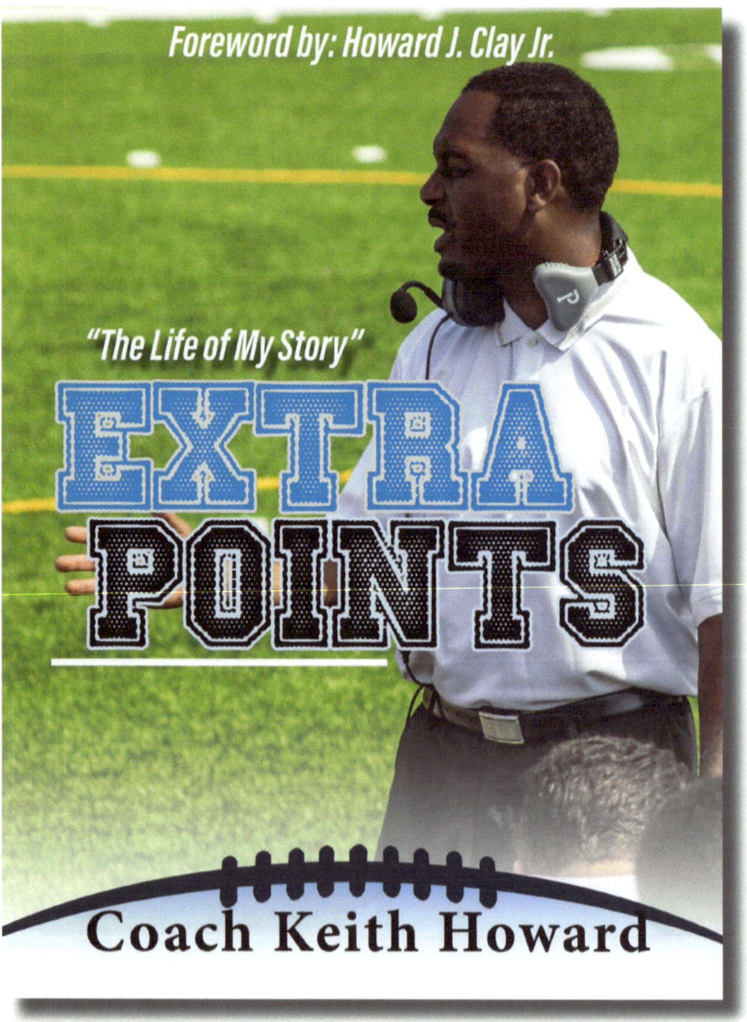

TWO

TWO

B.O.S.S. Magazine

Keeping It
100
with
Dr. G. I. Berry
@trsnovel

Dear G.I. Berry, I asked this girl out and was really pleased when she said yes. I liked the way she looked and of course wanted to have sex with her and thought she was up for the same thing. But after going out a couple of times, realized that she expected me to open the car door for her, and pay for all her meals and drinks. But when she kept rejecting me I knew she had to go. I think she should have known better than to expect a college student to want to be in a relationship or be her meal ticket. I know plenty of girls who would give it up for a packet of Ramen noodles, so I'm not desperate. I sat her down and told her that I wanted to have fun and didn't want to see her anymore unless she gave it up. I told her it's 2016 and not 1816! She didn't argue with me, just told me it was fine because it was clear we wanted different things, she wasn't upset and wished me the best. I see her around campus and she has clearly moved on from me. Now I feel used and angry about the time and money I wasted on her. I want to call to let her know that she should give me back the money I spent on her but know it's really to hear her voice. I can't stop thinking about her. Do you think I should try to get her back?

Sincerely, Used and Confused.

◇◇◇

Why? Why do you want her back? Is it because you feel she has gotten one over on you and you want revenge? Or is it because she behaved in a manner which challenged you and it has proven to be a surprising but attractive quality? You have used the word thought several times and so it suggests to me that you may not have clarified with her what you expected from your encounter in the beginning. Why did you go to the trouble of asking someone out? Explore your motives, be honest with yourself, reflect on your approach – Did you make the assumption that she wanted the same thing as you? What gave you that impression? Or did you expect her to read your mind telepathically? Unfortunately, not many of us have that talent and so we have to rely on using words to communicate what is going on in our minds. Communicating clearly requires not only

Photo credit: Institute of Education

courage, but also respect and trust. You may not like, or agree with someones response but it means you can create a platform from which to have an open honest discussion. If you had, it would have given her the option to accept or reject your offer (consequently, ensuring that you did not spent any unnecessary time or money on trying to get her into your bed). So the next question I want you to ask yourself, is why didnt you communicate what you wanted from her straight out? I understand there are plenty of phone apps which can deliver women who share your same goal, like pizza or as you say, for a bowl of Ramen noodles!!! No need for games or miscommunication. It is 2016, which means she is entitled to reject your offer if it was not what she wanted. You have to respect her position. You seem to be the one that needs to realize it is not 1816 and women can exercise their right to determine whether or not they want to have an encounter with you.I think you need to give some serious thought to why the demands she made on you forced you to see her as more than a live blanket or entertainment for the evening. You said you went out a couple of times – Why? Did her actions make you feel like a protector? Were you afraid you couldnt live up to her expectations? Or did she reflect your inadequacies so you reverted back to your demand/expectation for sex to avoid the emotions being with her evoked? My job is not to tell you what to think rather to give you things to think about. Neither am I here to tell you what to do. I want you to be empowered to make the best decision for you. Just know that every encounter we have should teach us something about ourselves. You had a powerful lesson that should tell you what you want. Your job is to figure it out in order to create a life filled with the things you want, rather than regrets of what you should or should not have done.

Dr. Gillian Berry, MSW, LICSW, LCSW-C is a licensed clinical social worker in the District of Columbia and the State of Maryland, with 25 years of experience. She is Director of Clinical Social Work Services and interim Director of The George Washington University Mental Health Services. She is author of The Righteous Sin and regular contributor to B.O.S.S magazine.

Hurt 2 Heal Inc.

Joyce Reed is a Chicago native, who developed her love for writing at the age of 10. That was her only way of communicating, so she felt she needed to write down her day to day events because she didn't know if she would make it to see another day. By the age of 23 she took everything that she wrote in her journals and notebooks and wrote a book **"Hurt Used To Live Here"** to help inspire others to write their own story. Everyone has a story but not everyone has the courage to speak out about it. Joyce stopped being ashamed and embarrassed of what people thought of her and realized that her life was bigger than her and she had a purpose. So who else better to tell her story, but her? At this point in her life she has so many things, both good and positive. She is courageous, she is bold, she is strong, she is a fighter, she is a believer, she is a mother, she is a winner, she is funny, she is ambitious, she is brave and she is a child of GOD!

Joyce had overcome so many challenges in her life that she sometimes wanted to give up and take the easy way out, but GOD had other plans for her because every attempt to end her life was unsuccessful. She would sometimes wonder why she was on this earth. She would wonder, why all of these negative things transpiring in her life andit seemslike every day it gets more and more challenging? Now looking back, Joyce sees that every obstacle that was put in her path was a challenge to make her stronger and wiser. She is here for a reason and now that she has faith and believes she will continue her work as she walks this earth daily, healthy, and able. She will continue to follow her path and trust that his way is the right way and he will never steer her wrong. Deuteronomy 31:6 "Be strong and courageous. Do not be afraid or terrified because of them, for the LORD your God goes with you; he will never leave you nor forsake you."Even though her childhood

was taken from her at the age of 8, she will continue to forgive so she can be forgiven. She is not proud of her past, but she is proud of the woman she's become. Her mission is to motivate and give courage to others to also tell their stories.Joyce Reed started a Movement called **"I am UR Voice"** and to join the movement all you have to do is create a board/post, share it online, releasing your fears and #iamurvoice. For example, "You took my innocence #iamurvoice, I cried but my voice went silent #iamurvoice.My duty, as a survivor of sexual assault, domestic violence, and mental abuse, is to be the voice for others who have been impacted by different forms of abuse. My calling in life is to share my story and be an encouraging voice for others to not be ashamed and embarrassed of what someone did to us. I am no longer ashamed to say that I am a survivor of being molested, raped, and fondled 6 times in my life, being raped by my father at a tender age, having both of my children out of rape, being homeless, losing my family in 1 year, being in a domestic violence relationship, and thinking that a black eye was love. After trying to commit suicide 3 times is when I found my calling and my purpose in life. My life is bigger than me and I want to continue my journey and with your support it will help me get closer to my goal in being the voice for others.Joyce then went on and started a nonprofit with the mission to bring awareness to the community and allow men and women to have a voice and speak out about what they were once afraid of.

Hurt 2 Heal Inc. is an organization hat offers a voice for individuals impacted by all forms of abuse. *Our mission is to renew awareness and support the healing and restoration process of individuals impacted by abuse, by providing the necessary resources and tools needed to promote individuals and family healing.*

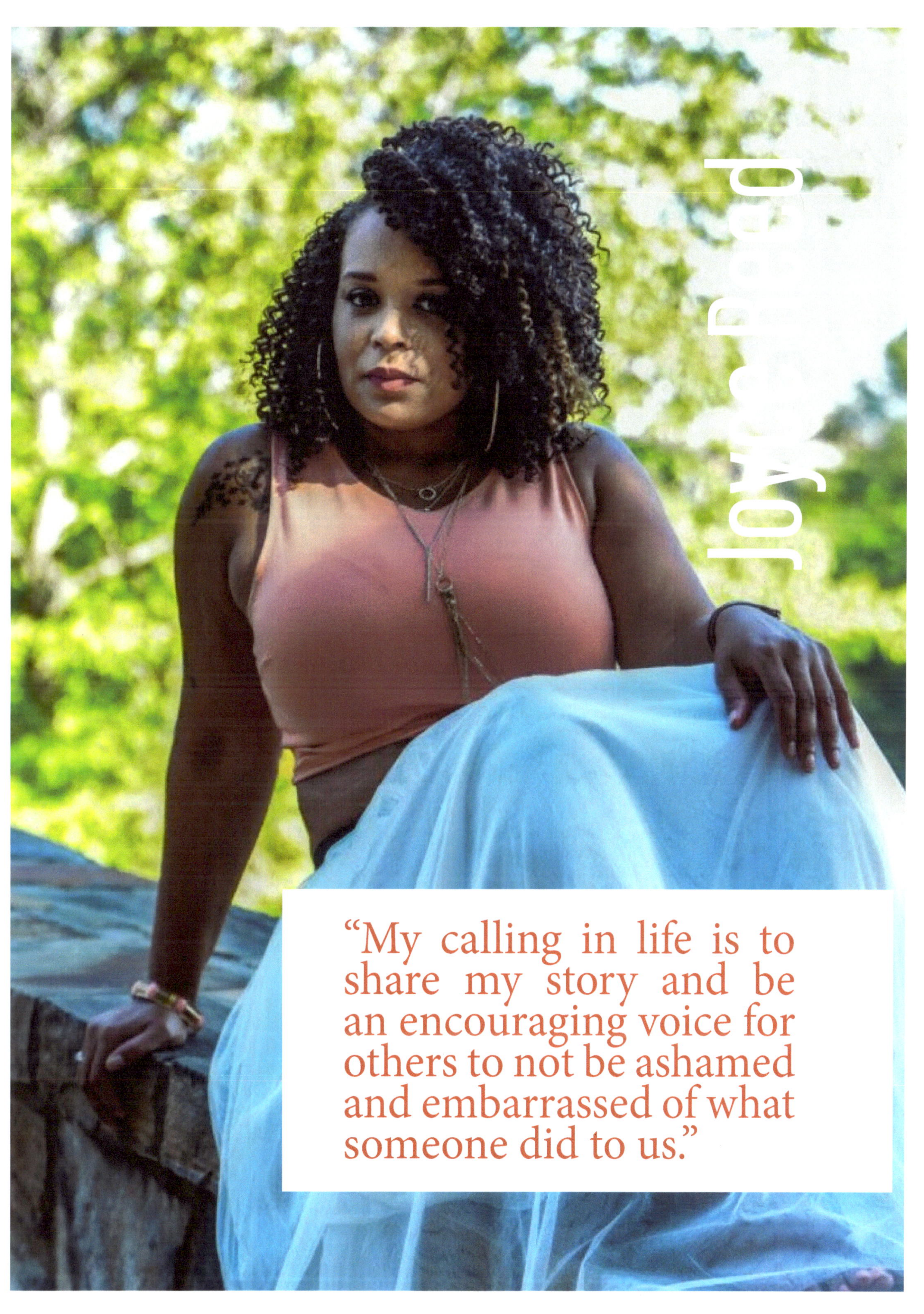

Joyce Reed
"My calling in life is to share my story and be an encouraging voice for others to not be ashamed and embarrassed of what someone did to us."

"3 Keys for Success"

Kamil McFadden

Photo credit: TEENplicity

Interview by Drdesha
(Twitter/Instagram: @Drdesha)

Jovial, diligent worker, and humble. These aren't necessarily the perceived characteristics of today's young celebrities, but they're imminently present within Disney's K.C. Undercover star, Kamil McFadden. While supporting his brother's football camp (Kimario McFadden), I was able to gain insight on his work ethic and I wanted to share three keys of success that Kamil shared with me. He is definitely wise beyond his years!

1.   Your Education Is A Priority.
Kamil credits his mother for instilling in him the importance of education. He recalls when he first knew that acting was what he wanted to do. His mother made sure to let him know that finishing his homework and finishing school was non negotiable.

2.   Prepare for the NOs and the YES.
Kamil was aware of the fact that in the entertainment industry you have to be able to work past the rejections. There will be no's. Yet you have to remember to continue improving and working at your craft, because when you get that one YES, it will all be worth it.

3.   There is a time to Work and for Play.
Kamil, even at an early age, balanced his school work and career. He remembers being in the fourth grade and heading out to California for a few weeks and still being right on top of his homework. Even now, he likes to have fun but knows that there are times for work and play.

To stay up to date with Kimario McFadden, follow him on Twitter & Instagram: @Kamil_McFadden

"Is it Politics As Usual?"
Thaddeus Walls

President of Northern Kentucky Democrats, Secretary for Kentucky Young Democratics & Civic Engagement Specialist for Urban League Young Professionals of Southwest Ohio.

Is important to vote anymore? That's the initial slippery slope, we are reared with the notion of using voting to fortify our voices and interests. Unfortunately, in America voting is just one cog in harnessing the voice or collective will of the people. Voting is important; however it is useless if neither the electorate nor campaigns engage in a constructive manner. Furthermore, in order to amplify the potential impact of voting, more attention should be drawn to the local issues & ballot races in our respective individual communities. Voting is not the total Alpha & Omega vehicle for starting change in our community; it is merely one component in the power structure of our society. There' s voting, lobbying, writing your elec elected officials, donating your time or money to a cause or issue, etc. Injustice is a very real thing, but until we understand how power works in America it' ll be a continuous circle of repetition. Racial tension in America has caused many to turn to protesting. There is no ' right' way to handle race issues in 2016. The issues that face America are the same issues that have plagued this country since its inception, the application or rather the lack of application of rights and laws applied toward people of color. Due to the Romanization of the Civil Rights Movement many believe that protesting is the ' only' way to cause change. Have we made progress? Incremental perhaps, but our country still has much further to go. Protesting is good for creating awareness, but Stokely Carmichael once said, "In order for non-violence to work the oppressor must have a conscious". As a people it will take more than protesting to achieve change, but it is a quicker action to organize.   Does wealth play a factor the issues that plague the disenfranchised? Very much so. Wealth amplifies the response of government to community problems. The response of our country to the heroin epidemic is a far cry from the same reaction to the crack epidemic. Also, wealth makes the difference in regards to how the average American interacts with the very people that are supposed to represent their interests.

So what does being an activist in 2016 mean? Everybody can play a role, however we all are operating in different spaces, and not everything is meant to be posted or shared or if you have enough time to point out what somebody isn't doing. Then it is up to YOU if you are the one not doing anything. In my opinion being an activist in 2016 is simply using one' s gifts, talents, or network in order to bring awareness in regards to unequal application of justice. Let's meet people where they are first before we tell them what's good for them, because that's why people don't vote, you wouldn't like it if somebody ran up to you trying to tell you about your story and they know nothing about your experience in America. When it comes to this year's presidential election, what is there to consider? Make sure to do your own research in order to draw your own conclusions. It' s not the only election worth paying attention. Let's do better by holding us all accountable and demand better from our electorate, political parties and candidates. Much is at stake and remember this is real life, not just polls & MSNBC. GET INVOLVED.

JUMP Africa

Story Written by:Yennenga Adanya,
Educational Specialist and Author of
Rear Them Well: Practical Tools for Raising a Genius

Anyone who knows me, knows that I have desired to visit Africa for a pretty long time. As many other African American children, I hadn't learn about my rich ancestral history, until I met one of my favorite college professors, eventually mentor in grad school, Dr. Asa Hilliard III, who was well known for his annual tours of Africa. It was through his teachings that I learned about Ancient African culture, traditions, and history. He would urge us to learn as much as we could about our traditions and history, proclaiming that it is the key to our liberation here in America. I not only wanted to learn about these traditions and history, I wanted to witness them first hand. I was not fortunate enough to join one of his tours before he passed away, but I never gave up hope that I would eventually make my way there and even take others. I continued to include the journey on my vision board and speak my

desire every chance that presented itself. One of those chances presented itself at a global networking event I attended. I introduced myself, my area of expertise, and proceeded to explain my desire to establish a program that would afford young people, who would otherwise not have the opportunity, the opportunity to travel to Africa, and for a period of time reside there amongst a community, attend school, serve the community in some way, and more importantly seek and find historical traditions and cultural practices that they can identify with and adopt to positively affect their and their families' lives. My reflection caught the attention of a colleague of mine and he said to me "I must introduce you to my brother Fotemah Mba. He's from Cameroon and is doing great work through his organization JUMP Africa." He proceeded to briefly explain that this brother had developed a relationship with Books for Africa and had shipped over large crates of educational materials and built libraries and learning centers in Africa. Sounded like my type of work! Just like that, he made a call and turned to

me and said he's on the way! Now usually, often being a perfectionist, I would be apprehensive with such a last minute meeting, but I wasn't at all. I jetted to my car grabbed my book, resume, card, and anything else I could find that would make a strong enough impression to compel him to invite me on the next trip! Twenty minutes later, we were chatting, sharing our passions, mission, and vision and low and behold, A KINDRED SPIRIT. The synergy was strong and clear. "When can I come?!" 3 months later I was booking my ticket, sending off my visa application

and researching, "Things to bring on your trip to Africa". The journey had begun. I was on my way to Africa! Although Fotemah explained what we would be doing during our trip, distributing materials and teacher training, I consciously made an effort not to develop any expectations around the trip. I clearly knew that the goal was impact, but aside from that I wanted to stay wide open to the experience. I didn't know what to expect with living quarters (from the questions I got from a number of people I found that the stereotype of huts and bare bodies

still prevail), wasn't sure how I would be received (I lost count how many times I was told not to be surprised if I was treated poorly because I'm American or because I am "light skinned"), and a day didn't go by without a reminder of the "malaria scare". Despite it all I stayed open to the experience, no matter what, and I am SO GLAD I did. Fotemah was the best host one could have on their first trip to Africa and his hospitality never ceased even until now. No matter how hard we worked all day, him working 2 times harder sometimes, being that he was not only there to distribute materials, get them set up, and train the staff on how to use them, but he was also putting out fires, handing out hugs and smiles, lending words of praise and encouragment, and keeping his mother updated on the progress throughout the whole process. He never complained and was on top of making sure we were as comfortable as possible. It was something to witness. In true Cameroonian fashion, he was getting it done! (After a few days there witnessing the EVERY DAY hard work of the locals, carrying large loads on their heads, building some of the most beautiful homes I've ever seen BY HAND, riding bikes towing a truck load UP HILL, I affectionately named Cameroon, "The land of making it happen!"). What was even more appreciated was that he also made a conscious effort to make sure our (the ambassadors who accompanied him) personal goals were met.

During our time there I was allowed to share my gifts and passion in training teachers. I implemented my "Awakening the Sleeping Giant," workshop with the teachers and staff and indeed these teachers were true giants! They produced the highest performing students in the nation. It became clear to me after observations that I was not there to teach them, I was there to celebrate them and encourage them to dig even deeper and reach even higher. The teachers were highly receptive and almost thirsty for what was being presented. I eventually learned through observation and surveying that there were many area that the teachers welcomed professional development in including, effective pedagogical practices for teaching children with learning disabilities. Unlike schools here, there is no apparent structured way in identifying students with learning disabilities or developing the teachers in this area so that they can be most effective in teaching them. What was impressive, and I made sure I highlighted this every chance I got, the teachers were still highly effective even with their children with apparent learning disabilities. What all of this did for me is affirm that there are still passionate teachers in this world and that with the right amount of will you can accomplish whatever goal you set. I have promised to contribute whatever I can to the

continued development of the teachers there starting with helping them to develop an effective system that will help identify students with learning disabilities and develop learning plans that will help the students succeed despite the struggles they may have. This article would be a novel if I was to express all of the lessons I learned during my journey to Cameroon with Fotemah and JUMP Africa.

One of the most impactful ones was lessons about the importance of and value in family and legacy. This is mostly the line of conversation between him and I as we traveled. He spoke about his family, their legacy, and his sense of responsibility to keep that legacy alive. He gave us the privilege to meet his family and visit his family home and village, and while we were there, explained so many beautiful commitments that families stay true to. With dignity and much humility he made his rounds visiting family, friends, and elders who affectionately calls him "Pa" meaning father/elder because he upholds who his Pa was and what his Pa did for them when he was still here. He never ceased to capture teachable moments (and shots, I call him the money shot man) throughout the entire trip, moments that I will never forget. Fotemah has established an organization that does not only collect resources and ship them to little old towns that need our help. He has established an organization that give communities that added push for them to dig even deeper than they already do on a daily and press forward, because there are people watching them and rooting for them and her to support. I am so grateful that I am one of those people. I am proud to be a JUMP Africa ambassador and I urge you to only step up and be one as well if you have the heart of a servant and the tenacity of a Cameroonian, the Land of MAKE IT HAPPEN!

For more information about JUMP Africa, visit www.jumparica.org

Latosha Williams

Coaching Services

Life Coach

Life coaching assists individuals to produce change in their environment, moving them from where they are to where they want to be. By having an engaging conversation that empowers the client to get what they desire by thinking and performing more resourcefully. As a result, new possibilities are opening up.

Education

Education coaching can equip individuals with the skills necessary to flourish and obtain future goals. In turn, enabling them to triumph over any obstacles they might encounter. The sections address the best ways for students to manage stress, obtain high grade achievement, and sustain motivation.

Development

Development coaching focus on a person values, strengths, and resourcefulness. "A person core foundation is leading development for success in achieving any goal. Whatever the mind of man can conceive and believe, it can achieve" (Napoleon Hill). Through compassion, patience and a confidence that everyone can change, a good coach dismantles road blocks people place in front of themselves.

Parenting & Kids Coaching

Parenting and Kids Coaching is enhances the natural skills parent already possess. The section creates assistance to clients when assess their own situations. Enabling them to think and act more resourcefully about how to improve problem as they arise. Better parenting skills will enhance children development for their future. Therefore, parents will better guide children and helping them discover their true identity and their inborn strengths. This is the key to parenting them positively.

At a early age I was diagnosed with epilepsy. The doctors said I would never be normal. The doctor said I would have a learning disabilities. However, just look at me today. This moment is for anyone who knows they are destined for greatness no matter what anyone says about them. You speak and shape your future! Whatever your mind believes your heart can achieve. If you know that you're bigger than what others say about you, then it is your duty to likethis page and share your story. Love you all. Love all your disabilities and abilities.

Contact information
Latosha Williams
404-902-2008
Facebook:Tosha Williams
Instagram: peoplemovingforward
Youtube:Moving Forward
Website:peoplemovingforward.org

People Moving Forward.org
A PROFESSIONAL LIFE COACH EMPOWERING INDIVIDUALS TO ACHIEVE LIFE PURPOSE!

B.O.S.S.
Entrepreneurs
on the move!

"The Dangers of Operating in the Comfort Zone"

Phillip Brazile

CEO of Philosophy Media Group

A philosopher once said, "The best way to get something done is to begin." The first step is a milestone to success. For so many people, the first step is the easiest and the hardest at the same time.   We all have been in this place of comfort. We have gotten the brochures in the mail about destination vacations, and we thought to ourselves, *I am going to save up money so I can go take a cruise...* Then next to the brochure lies a stack of bills, and you quickly forget about the dream vacation brochure with your desired trip. We spent many days in our minds of thinking out dreams and visions, and even attended vision board parties and managed to scribble down a couple of typical goals. Then like always, reality comes with its distractions and wakes us up out of the "dream" world. The word dream itself is defined as the act of contemplating the possibility of doing something. Dreams only act as visual to the future often what to do and expect. However, so many of us let our visuals stay limited due to our comfort zone. Not pursing your dreams, goals, and ambitions is surrendering to fear. I once had a college professor, who became a professor at the age of 55. One lesson she taught me was timing and opportunity. She often spoke about how she spent thirty years working at a factory. She thought she was at her prime, so she brought her house, marriage, and even built a 401k. Then one day she woke up and realized she was not living out her heart's desires. She just became another person working to work but no purpose behind it. She realized her desires to be a mathematic professor, retired, and enrolled in a community college, and earned her way up to receiving a Doctorate degree. A light bulb went off for me. *I thought, Wow, why work a job for all of these years and no purpose?* Why wait to get to a certain point in your life to reach out for your dreams?To get out of the comfort zone, you have to get comfortable with being uncomfortable. It is not going to be easy to ask your relatives for money to help finance your business. It is not going to be comfortable taking a pay cut, so you can go to school at night. It might not be comfortable struggling to where you want to be. Realize where you are and your potential. You must now align yourself to go for something bigger. You have the entry level positon, reach for a management position. You have the car, the house, but let's pay off the debt. Your next step of achievement is not a stopping point. Take time to celebrate, then regain focus and stay out of the comfort zone.

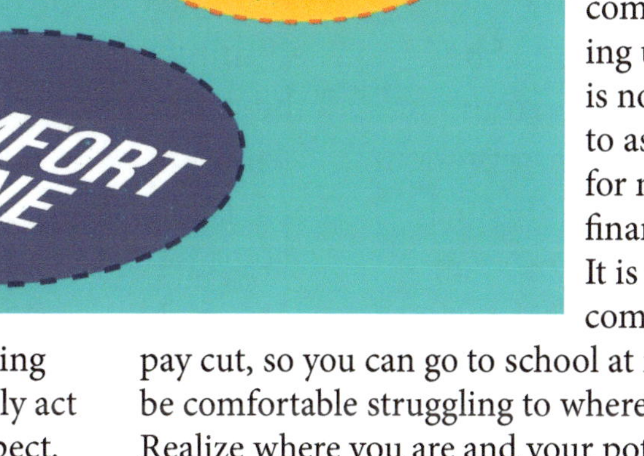

Photo Credit: Redzonemarketing

Montina Portis

Montina Portis is the founder of the Atlanta Video Studio, a place where creatives and non-creatives can tell their stories, build their brands, and disrupt the market using online video. She opened the video studio in Atlanta so that entrepreneurs could produce high-quality, professional videos at an affordable price. Montina went from living in a homeless shelter at 19 to graduating with her master's, retiring from the largest I.T. financial company in the United States in 2014 and founding the nation's first video marketing company founded by a woman that focuses exclusively on marketing for attorneys. Her life story proves that all things are possible to those that work hard and believe in achieving success. She is also the author of YouTube Secrets Revealed, How to Market Your Law Firm Online, and she has over 4 million views on her YouTube channel and has produced over 500 videos for attorneys that have generated more than 100,000 views.

Through her famous personal transformation experiences, and frequent appearances on Network TV shows including "The Chew", Fox News, ABC, CBS, and NBC. Montina inspires millions of people to be superstars in life and business and live amazing lives.

To schedule your FREE interview as a guest on Montina's show, In The Studio go to ---> http://AtlantaVideoStudio.com

C.H. Miller

"How Purpose Brought Him Back To That Place Called School "

C.H. Miller, formerly known as Cameron H. Miller, is an Empowerment Speaker, Actor, Producer, and now Author. He is on an intense mission truly living life according to purpose while empowering others to do the same thing! There is so much to share about C.H. Miller but for the purpose of this article we are going to focus more on his journey of how finding his purpose brought him back to the very place he never thought he would return. You know that exciting place that if permitted, shall catapult your thinking alongside lifelong knowledge and experiences; that place we call college. Originally born and raised in Las Vegas, Nevada, C.H. Miller has worked in the entertainment industry for nearly 20 years. Like many, his tenure has been multifaceted from being a 1st assistant production accountant, an actor, a correspondent bringing you the hottest celebrity interviews from the red carpets for the Golden Globes, American Music Awards, BET Awards, and more. He is the former COO of Studio 11 Films, based out of Atlanta, GA. During his tenure there, the company launched the directorial debut of LisaRay McCoy's highly rated international film, *Skinned*, which was recently nominated for an AMAA Award. C.H. Miller has resided and made his mark in the following cities, Hollywood (CA), Atlanta (GA), and New York (NY), later returning back to his hometown, Las Vegas (NV). He shares, that it was only 2 ½ years ago during his stay in Atlanta that he found himself "standing on the balcony of a tall high-rise building, with one leg over the edge, ready to end it all." It was at that very moment, he decided to live. He made the conscious choice to search and find out why on earth God had him here. He needed to know what his true purpose was and how did his many talents come into play. For him, it seemed as if he was running in circles and what seemed real

were lies. But that night he made a choice, and so his quest begun in search for the real reason why he was born. It was during this quest that he transitioned from focusing on acting to more on film producing and presently focusing particularly on empowering, coaching, and speaking life into others. Like other millennials, living life according to purpose is what he is passionate about and moves him to release the greatness in which he already possesses inside of him. As C.H. Miller began to birth his purpose, his desire to know God's word better for himself rapidly prompted growth in a spiritual aspect as well as maturate. Before he knew it, he was enrolling in Kairos School of Ministry, which is a satellite campus for Northwest University; one of the top 10 Christian Universities, and began majoring in Ministry Leadership. Although he wished he could say it is quite easy, he can't. Now in his mid 30s, focusing on being an amazing father to an 11-year-old girl and a 19-year-old young man, he remains extremely busy. Additionally, he is a profound advocate for strengthening and giving back to urban communities, continuously serving in leadership positions; including,

paving the way for young and future leaders in the areas of acting, film producing, and civic engagement.   Even though his plate is overflowing, attending school full-time, his journey must continue because he has accepted it, and he constantly reminds himself of his responsibility and purpose. Now C.H. Miller, formerly known as Cameron H. Miller, abbreviated his name as a symbol of reinventing and rebirthing who he really is and who he is destined to become. School is the last place he thought he would return, nonetheless excited, as he never realized how liberating the process would be. He not only begun to understand the Word for himself but he found himself. Even more importantly, he found a reason to live, and with a purpose. You are encouraged to follow C.H. Miller as he continues to birth and develop his purpose. A genuine be your own success story, because he discovered that he already had greatness on the inside of him, which allowed him to be empowered and now he is on a mission to help others release their greatness and walk in their purpose too!

About the Author: Trina-Marie Phinizy is a brand manager, consultant and published photographer. She believes in

designing your life and helps you to achieve your desires via marketing yourself through personal branding but with a purpose. You can find out more about her at http://Trina-Marie.com and on most social media sites @TrinaMariePhoto. Picture it, design it, and strategize! Believe and don't give up! Because you too, deserve to have a picture perfect life!

Written by: Trina-Marie Phinizy/ TM Branding & ConsultingSocial

Media Handlers:
Facebook (Bus): http://facebook.com/CHMillerSpeaks
Twitter: @CHMillerSpeaks
Instagram: @CHMillerSpeaks
Snapchat: @CHMillerSpeaks
Youtube: @CHMillerSpeaks
Website: www.CHMillerSpeaks